THE Greatest Gift

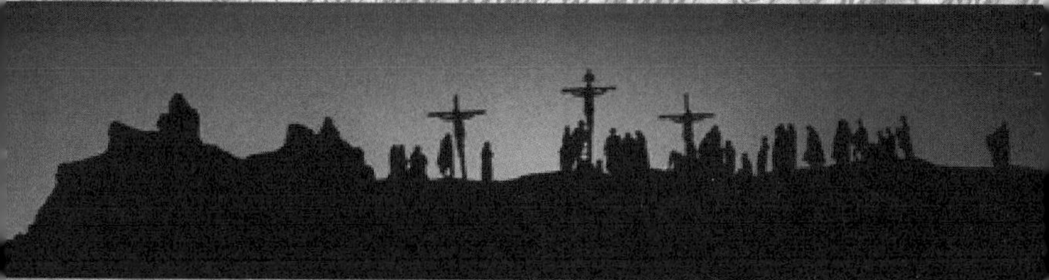

God's Amazing Grace

Amazing Grace

Amazing grace,
how sweet the sound,
That saved a wretch like me!
I once was lost,
but now am found,
Was blind, but now I see.

'Twas grace that taught
my heart to fear,
And grace my fears relieved;
How precious did that
grace appear,
The hour I first believed

THE
Greatest
Gift

God's Amazing Grace

HAL LINDSEY

WESTERN FRONT
PUBLISHING

The Greatest Gift:
God's Amazing Grace

By Hal Lindsey

Western Front, Ltd., Publishing Company
Palos Verdes, California

ISBN 1-888848-34-0

Western Front, Ltd.

Scriptures quoted in this book are from the
New American Standard Bible (NASB),
unless otherwise noted.

Editorial direction and design by Koechel
Peterson & Associates, Minneapolis,
Minnesota

Printed in the U.S.A.

Contents

see. ❧ 'Twas grace that taught my heart to fear, ❧ A

ear ❧ The hour I first believed. ❧ Through many

ce hath brought me safe thus far, ❧ And grace will lead

ord my hope secures: ❧ He will my shield and portion b

shall fail, ❧ And mortal life shall cease, ❧ I shall po

d shall soon dissolve like snow, ❧ The sun refuse to shine,

r mine. ❧ When we've been there ten thousand years, ❧

's praise ❧ Than when we'd first begun. ❧ Amazing g

❧ I once was lost, but now am found, ❧ Was blind be

❧ And grace my fears relieved. ❧ How precious did

any dangers, toils and snares, ❧ I have already come.

ed me home. ❧ The Lord has promised good to me, ❧

be, ❧ As long as life endures ❧ Yea, when this fl

ll possess, within the veil, ❧ A life of joy and peace.

u. ❧ But God, who called me here below, ❧ Shall

❧ Bright shining as the sun. ❧ We've no less days

grace! How sweet the sound ❧ That saved a wretch

HOW I MET
"GRACE"

Amazing grace,
how sweet the sound,
That saved a wretch like me!
I once was lost,
but now am found,
Was blind,
but now I see.

~CAPTAIN JOHN NEWTON

he fog was so thick I could not see the bow of my boat on the Mississippi River. Despite the horrid conditions I knew I had to ferry several oil drilling crew members across the river.

9

At the age of twenty-five I was a devout pagan and a tugboat captain who worked hard and played even harder in New Orleans.

Quickly I tried to start the generator that powered the radar. I tried once and it wouldn't start. I tried to prime it—nothing. Without radar you have no idea what's happening on that old river. Without a generator, I also didn't have compressed air to operate the signal horn.

The Mississippi was extremely dangerous in good weather, but in this kind of weather it was absolutely spooky. Most captains would call a trip across the river under these conditions, without a radar or a signal horn, attempted suicide.

"We're not going anywhere tonight," I announced after the third futile attempt to start the generator.

"To hell with the fog," the head tool pusher retorted. "Just do your job and get us across the river.

We have an emergency out at the drilling platform and we've got to get there."

"Okay, okay—it's your necks," I replied with a bit of false bravado.

So with only a compass and a stopwatch, we shoved off. When we got to about the middle of the mile-and-a-quarter-wide river, my heart almost froze. I heard the sound of the huge ship's engine coming straight toward us. I heard the steamship's horn blaring the danger signal as the river pilot picked us up on his radar. I couldn't even see the bow of my boat, much less the other ship.

I pulled the throttle back and hopelessly stared into the blackness. I thought, "God, I wish I could've found You." Something like an invisible force caused me to spin the helm (steering wheel) to the right. We immediately hit a glancing blow to the huge ship, just behind the bow. We were inches away from being hit broadside.

I slowed the boat down. We were lost in the fog. My prefigured compass heading and speed settings were useless. By a miracle we dodged away from another ship and ran aground on the other side of the river—not too far from my dock.

I wasn't really afraid while all the action was going on, but later that night I got a little shaken. I wondered, "If there is a God, is He trying to tell me something?" My life began to flash before me like a video on fast-forward. I remembered the words of an elderly gentleman from a mission off Times Square. His words so shook me that I determined to find out if Jesus Christ was for real or not.

BACK TO THE BEGINNING

My life's journey began in Houston, Texas. My folks weren't churchgoers. If my mother on rare occasions decided to attend, she would drag me along—usually over my objections.

I remember a particular Sunday morning I

decided to visit a church and the pastor said, "If you want to become a Christian, walk down to the front."

I was only twelve, but I was sincere about wanting to know God. I walked forward.

As a result of what I learned in that church in the next few months, I came to the conclusion that life was like a giant balancing scale. If I did more good things than bad things, the scale would tip in my favor and I'd make it to heaven. But I already saw that the scale was tipping heavily in the wrong direction.

My commitment didn't last. God didn't seem real. I learned very little about Jesus, and He certainly wasn't real to me either. I never even heard the word grace.

When I was fifteen I wondered, "Why is life so complicated?" Conflicts at home were erupting into volcanoes, and my personal life was becoming a tangled net of emotions.

Even with the growing hostility, my heart somehow yearned for peace with God. I found another church and walked the aisle when the invitation was given. Like a vaccination, I was hoping it would "take" this time.

They advised me of all the "don'ts" I had to obey to be a Christian: "Don't smoke, drink, dance, fornicate, gamble, or go to the movies." If only these people would have told me about salvation by grace through faith.

Again, I began to drift away from church. The harder I tried to be good, the more I fouled up. Guilt drove me away and peer pressure finally prevailed.

In my quest to find God, I went with a friend to yet another church. For the third time, I responded to the invitation, signed the membership card, and was baptized.

Another false start. Everybody wanted me to join their church, but I just wanted to know about

Jesus—and nobody seemed to be able to tell me how to know Him.

I reasoned that I had done my part, but God didn't do His. As a bitter young man, I dove headlong into the pool of hedonism. At the University of Houston I enrolled in "Partying 101" and for two years majored in booze and sex.

AN UNEXPECTED ENCOUNTER

I didn't want to think about the war that was escalating in Korea, but Uncle Sam had other ideas. Who wanted to trudge in the mud with the North Koreans? Not me. I rushed out to join the U.S. Coast Guard.

I was soon sent to the Coast Guard Academy in Connecticut. On one of my frequent weekend visits to New York City, I drank up all my money on Friday night. So my buddy and I decided to stand on Times Square until some fellow sailor came by and loaned us some money.

About the mid-afternoon I spotted a big sign just off Times Square that said, "Free Food!" A smaller sign beneath it said, "Jesus Saves." I laughed and said, "Hey, let's get those Holy Joes to feed us. They ought to be good for something!"

Eating was easy. Exiting proved to be a bit more difficult. A well-dressed man in his late fifties blocked the door and said, "Are you a Christian, young man?"

"I hope so," I replied without blinking.

He didn't budge. "Sailor, I can tell by your answer that you are not a Christian."

I tried to brush off his remark, but he continued, "Sailor, it doesn't matter how bad or how good you've been. There is only one thing that matters. Do you understand that when Jesus hung on that cross, God put every sin you would ever commit on Him?"

I shoved him aside and laughed as my friend and I moved for the door. But I can still remember his final, cutting words. "Young man," he said, "you can reject me, but if you turn your back on God's gift of love and pardon, then His wrath will surely fall on you forever."

By God's grace, these very words came back to me after nearly being killed on the Mississippi River.

The Coast Guard transferred me to the bawdy city of New Orleans, where I sank even deeper into a godless, anything-for-a-thrill lifestyle.

The first quarter-century of my life can be summed up as a search to fill a growing sense of emptiness which nothing physical or sensual seemed to fulfill. I began to search for something—anything—that might explain why the things I thought would make me happy didn't.

One sleepless night I reached to the bottom of my seabag and pulled out an old Gideons New

Amazing grace! How sweet the sound & That sav...

Was blind, but now I see. & Twas grace that taugh...

...recious did that grace appear & The hour I first beli...

...come. & Tis grace hath brought me safe thus fa...

...His Word my hope secures; & He w...

...when this flesh and heart shall fail, & And mortal life...

...below, & Shall be forever mine. & When we've been t...

...o less days to sing God's praise & Than when we'd f...

...aved a wretch like me! & I once was lost, but now am...

...ought my heart to fear, & And grace my fears relieved,

...believed. & Through many dangers, toils and snares...

...r, & And grace will lead me home. & The Lord h...

...will my shield and portion be, & As long as life end...

...he sun... & But G... called...

...wretch like me! ☙ ...once was lost, but now am found

my heart to fear, ☙ And grace my fears relieved; ☙

...d. ☙ Through many dangers, toils and snares, ☙

☙ And grace will lead me home. ☙ The Lord

...my shield and portion be, ☙ As long as life endures

...all cease, ☙ I shall possess, within the veil, ☙

The sun refuse to shine, ☙ But...

...ten thousand years, ☙ Bright shining as the sun, ☙

...begun. ☙ Amazing grace! How sweet the sound ☙

...und, ☙ Was blind, but now I see. ☙ 'Twas grace

☙ How precious did that grace appear ☙...

I have already come, ☙ 'Tis grace hath brought me

...promised good to me, ☙ ...Word my hope secures

...Yea, when this flesh and heart shall fail, ☙...

...and peace. ☙ The world...

...That saved...

Testament. I opened the pages to the beginning of the New Testament and started reading about the life of Jesus.

When I reached the fifth chapter of Matthew, I got discouraged. I was about to close the book forever when I flipped over to the Gospel of John, chapter three. Jesus was having a conversation with a man who was filled with questions. His name was Nicodemus. I thought, "This fellow seems to be similar to me."

Christ told him, *"Except a man be born again, he cannot see the Kingdom of God"* (John 3:3 KJV).

God's Holy Spirit began to work on me. I thought, "Oh, I wish I could be born again and start from scratch with a clean slate." Suddenly it hit me that I could be born again by simply believing that what Jesus did on the cross was for Hal Lindsey. I looked up and said, "God, if You are real, then show me how to believe."

In the back of that Gideons Bible were instructions on how to become a Christian. It quoted Revelation 3:20, *"Behold I stand at the door and knock; if anyone hears My voice and opens the door, I will come in to him, and will dine with him and he with Me."*

I said, "God, if this is true, I want Jesus Christ to come into my life and forgive me. If He can do that, then I accept Him right now."

When I woke up the next morning I was surprised to find myself reaching for the Bible. For the first time the Scriptures began to have meaning.

Changes began to happen in my life. Instead of heading for a drink, I found myself heading for my cabin to read God's Word. I didn't talk about it much, but the change in my lifestyle was so obvious to the crew that they became worried about me, as did the rest of my friends.

Six months had passed and I realized that if I was to grow as a Christian, I needed to get away from the hedonistic influence of the New Orleans scene. I headed for Houston, my hometown.

I began attending church and soon found myself studying the Scriptures almost six to eight hours every day—plus holding a full-time job. My parents enjoyed having me back home, but were worried that I was being consumed by "religion."

"What has happened to you?" my dad finally asked. "Can you help me understand the change?"

I told my father what had happened. That night, in the living room of our family home, my father asked Jesus to come into his heart and be his Savior.

My mother was a believer but struggled with her daily Christian life. It wasn't long, however, until Jesus became very personal and real to her.

One day God showed me His plan for my life. I was reading the account of Moses at the burning bush. God spoke to me and said, "You are going to be another bush through which I'm going to speak."

I was terrified of speaking in public. I said, "Lord, if You want me to preach, it's going to take a miracle." But when I read those words and realized how God used Moses, I said, "Lord, I'm Yours."

Before long I was asked to be the substitute teacher for an adult Bible class in Sunday school. What an experience! As long as I kept my mind on the Word, I had confidence. But when I thought about my speaking, I nearly fainted.

After the class a woman asked if she could speak with me. "Young man," she said, "I believe God has singled you out to teach His Word far and wide someday, but your grammar is really offensive. Nobody is going to want to listen to you."

That didn't come as any surprise to me. But what she said next did. "I'm an English teacher," she said. "If you'll come twice a week to my home, I'll teach you proper grammar." I accepted the offer, and within one year she brought me from third grade grammar to college level.

The call of God was becoming stronger every day. I prayed, "Lord, if it is possible, I would like to study at a seminary."

On the surface, it was impossible. I was a college dropout and had no religious credentials. I set my sights on Dallas Theological Seminary. As I mailed my application to Dallas I took a deep breath.

Within two weeks I received a letter that read: "Congratulations. You have been accepted as a student at Dallas Theological Seminary."

"Hallelujah!" I shouted. "The miracle has happened!"

I've been in the Lord's work for more than 40 years now, and by the grace of God I've seen many miracles worked in and through me.

Now if the Lord, by His amazing grace, could untangle the threads of my life and use me to write books that have touched the lives of millions of people around the world, I know He can do wonders for you, too. Just as God turned Simon, the impetuous vacillator, into Peter, the Rock; and Saul, the ultimate legalist, into Paul, the champion of grace; so He delights in taking ordinary people and creating something extraordinary out of them.

All Christians are "unfinished products" in the hands of a gracious God. Some of the worst sins I have committed have been after salvation. But God's grace taught me to believe His promises of forgiveness and to get up and trust Him again.

Grace properly understood doesn't promote loose living.

David testified concerning the secret of his life with God, *"If you, O Lord, kept a record of sins, O Lord, who could stand? But with you there is forgiveness;*

therefore you are feared [reverently trusted]. *I wait for the Lord, my soul waits, and in his word I put my hope"* (Psalm 130:3-5 NIV).

If you think God is holding past sins against you, you simply cannot believe Him now. The false guilt, fed by *"the Accuser of the brethren,"* produces estrangement that will not let you believe His promises.

The reason God is able to deal with us in such amazing grace is the entire subject of this book. It was all provided for at great cost at the CROSS.

*"For of His fulness
we have all received,
and grace upon grace."*

~JOHN 1:16

Chapter
TWO

WHAT IN THE
WORLD IS WRONG
WITH MAN?

*F*rom the first book of the Old Testament to the last book of the New Testament, there is one consistent theme, and that is that God and man experience an alienation—a barrier—that man cannot remove and God says He already has. There's no use talking about who Jesus was or why He came until we first understand the nature of the barrier that exists between man and his God.

Picture, if you will, the first record we have of man's relationship with God. It was in a beautiful environment, and there was true fellowship and communication between God and man. Man was free to

27

do as he wanted. He was asked to do one thing—not to eat of a certain tree in the Garden. This was a test of man's trust in God's judgment and care for him. It was also a test of whether he wanted to continue in the relationship. The tree itself was not evil; it was the choice to disobey God that was evil.

Before Eve and then Adam decided to take a bite of that forbidden fruit, they had to believe a lie about God's character. They had to believe that God did not have their best interest at heart—that indeed He was keeping something from them that would make them godlike. The moment they disobeyed, an impossible barrier was raised between themselves and God. The wonderful relationship they had enjoyed with their Creator was instantly broken. Spiritual life died. They no longer had the kind of life that God has.

By this original act mankind erected four great barriers that hopelessly separate us from God. This wall of barriers is so impenetrable that all the religions, philosophies, idealisms, good works, and ingenuity of men can't tear it down.

But on the basis of grace alone, God Himself has torn down the barriers.

Let's look at the barriers first. Then we can fully appreciate what it cost God to abolish them!

Amazing grace! How sweet the sound ❧ That saved a

Was blind, but now I see. ❧ Twas grace that taught m

cious did that grace appear ❧ The hour I first believed

eady come; ❧ Tis grace hath brought me safe thus far,

od to me, ❧ His word my hope secures; ❧ He will

en this flesh and heart shall fail, ❧ And mortal life

d peace ❧ The world shall soon dissolve like snow,

ow, ❧ Shall be forever mine. ❧ When we've been there

days to sing God's praise ❧ Than when we'd first

a wretch like me! ❧ I once was lost, but now am fou

ght my heart to fear, ❧ And grace my fears relieved;

ieved. ❧ Through many dangers, toils and snares, ❧

❧ And grace will lead me home. ❧ The Lord has p

my shield and portion be, ❧ As long as life endures ❧

shall cease, ❧ I shall possess, within the veil, ❧ A li

The sun refuse to shine, ❧ But God, who called me

re ten thousand years, ❧ Bright shining as the sun, ❧

t begun. ❧ Amazing grace! How sweet the sound ❧

Chapter
THREE

BARRIER NUMBER ONE: GOD'S HOLY CHARACTER

he character of God is so flawless and the nature of man is so fallen that the very holiness of God becomes a barrier to man.

Now, before you say to yourself, "Well, it's God's fault, then, that man is alienated from Him; God needs to lower His standards if He wants to reconcile with man," we need to take a look at what the character of God is really like.

God's essence, or character, is made up of ten absolute attributes. God the Father, Son, and Holy

31

Spirit is: 1) Sovereign; 2) Righteous; 3) Just; 4) Love; 5) Eternal Life; 6) Omniscient; 7) Omnipresent; 8) Omnipotent; 9) Immutable; and 10) Veracity.

FIRST: GOD IS SOVEREIGN

God has a will. By Himself and with assistance from no one He makes decisions and policies and sets up principles. He has the right to do whatever He pleases.

The sovereignty of the Almighty was established before creation. *"Even from eternity I am He; and there is none who can deliver out of My hand; I act and who can reverse it?"* (Isaiah 43:13).

SECOND: GOD IS RIGHTEOUS

God is absolute virtue and perfection. He is the standard of all that is right. He is morally perfect without a shadow of deviousness. God is the standard by which all righteousness is measured. *"Righteous are You, O Lord, and upright are Your judgments"* (Psalm 119:137).

THIRD: GOD IS JUST

God is absolutely just. It's impossible for Him to do anything that's unfair either to Himself or to any creature. He executes perfect justice in accordance with His attribute of righteousness.

Moses said, *"He is the Rock, His work is perfect; for all His ways are justice, a God of truth and without injustice; righteous and upright is He"* (Deuteronomy 32:4 NKJV).

FOURTH: GOD IS LOVE

God is perfect, infinite love. It's given freely and without any consideration of the loveliness or merit of the object. It includes His enemies as well as His friends.

The Apostle John defined true love when he wrote, *"In this the love of God was manifested toward us, that God has sent His only begotten Son into the world, that we might live through Him. In this is love, not that we loved*

God, but that He loved us and sent His Son to be the propitiation [the satisfaction of the demands of God's justice] *for our sins"* (I John 4:9, 10 NKJV).

FIFTH: GOD IS ETERNAL LIFE

There has never been a time when God did not exist, and there never will be a time when He ceases to exist.

His changeless, permanent nature has no beginning and no end. *"Before the mountains were brought forth, or ever You had formed the earth and the world, even from everlasting to everlasting, You are God"* (Psalm 90:2). *"Jesus Christ is the same, yesterday, today, and forever"* (Hebrews 13:8 NKJV).

SIXTH: GOD IS OMNISCIENT

God possesses all knowledge. Nothing takes God by surprise.

This knowledge extends to even the smallest details. Jesus said that not even a sparrow can fall to the ground without the Father's knowledge (Matthew 10:29) and that *"the very hairs of your head are all numbered"* (Matthew 10:30).

SEVENTH: GOD IS OMNIPRESENT

The Creator God is able to permeate time and space and be personally present everywhere at all times. David comforted himself with this wonderful truth: *"Where can I go from your Spirit? Where can I flee from your presence? If I go up to the heavens, you are there; if I make my bed in the depths, you are there. If I rise on the wings of the dawn, if I settle on the far side of the sea, even there your hand will guide me, your right hand will hold me fast"* (Psalm 139:7-10 NIV).

He is personally present with everyone who seeks Him and worships Him.

EIGHTH: GOD IS OMNIPOTENT

God is all powerful. He has omnipotent power over nature, over the course of history, and over human life. God the Son not only created all things, but He continues to sustain all things by His almighty power.

When Job was in great distress he believed in His omnipotence: *"I know that You can do everything, and that no purpose of Yours can be withheld from You"* (Job 42:2 NKJV).

NINTH: GOD IS IMMUTABLE

This attribute means that God never changes in His nature or attributes. When He makes a promise or declares a truth, it will never change or not be fulfilled. Therefore we can believe that when He says He will do something, He will do it.

The same God who created the order of the universe still guides the affairs of man. He is constant and reliable. *"The counsel of the Lord stands forever, the plans of His heart from generation to generation"* (Psalm 33:11).

TENTH: GOD IS TRUTH OR VERACITY

God is absolute truth. Anything in word or deed that doesn't conform to what He reveals in His Word is not the truth. To know Him is to know reality.

The Lord is the essence of everything that is valid, authentic, and real. *"He is the Rock, His work is perfect; for all His ways are justice, a God of truth and without injustice; righteous and upright is He"* (Deuteronomy 32:4 NKJV).

There's not a person who's ever lived who could compare his life with God's character and say, "That's just the kind of person I am." According to James and Paul, we could keep every single point of the law and yet stumble in just one small area and that would be enough to disqualify us from enjoying fellowship with God for even a moment.

It's difficult for us to accept the absoluteness of this concept because of the relativistic thinking that predominates our lives. We can't fathom a holiness that won't bend "just a little" to accommodate our human weaknesses.

People tend to compare themselves with each other and see who comes the closest to a given mark. But "closeness" doesn't count with God. Coming close counts in darts, horseshoes, and hand grenades, but not in holiness. Interestingly, the root word for sin means "to miss the mark."

There is no possible way to achieve right standing with God by our own human efforts. There has to be some divine intervention by which man has supernaturally credited to him God's own righteousness.

Now, here was God's dilemma. Whereas the justice of God burned in wrath against man for outraging His holiness, God's love equally yearned to find a way to justly forgive him and bring him back into fellowship with Himself.

Chapter
FOUR

BARRIER
NUMBER TWO:
A DEBT OF SIN

o understand the nature of this debt of sin, we have to reach back into the practices of the Roman Empire's criminal courts. All Roman law assumed that every Roman citizen owed Caesar allegiance and obedience to his laws, and Roman justice was enforced swiftly.

If a man was found guilty of breaking the law and sentenced to prison, an itemized list was made of each infraction and its corresponding penalty. This list was, in essence, a record of how the man had failed to live up to the laws of Caesar. It was technically called a "Certificate of Debt." This Certificate of Debt was nailed to the prison cell door so anyone passing could tell the man had been justly condemned and see the limitations of his punishment.

When the man had served his time and was released, he would be handed the aged and tattered Certificate of Debt with the words "Paid in Full" written across it.

Man owes God perfect obedience to His holy laws.

Because of his inevitable disobedience, man has become an offense to the very character of God, and the eternal court of justice has pronounced the death sentence upon man.

Colossians chapter 2, verse 14, indicates that a Certificate of Debt was prepared against every person who would ever live, listing his failure to live in thought, word, and deed in accordance with the law of God. This death sentence has become a DEBT OF SIN which has to be paid, either by man or, if possible, someone qualified to take his place.

The Bible says that Jesus took our debt of sin and nailed it to His cross. The DEBT OF SIN has become another impossible barrier of the wall that separates God and man.

The greatest thing true Christianity has to offer is that it starts with the inside. The Holy Spirit takes up permanent residence inside of us. He gives us new motivation, new hope, and new power for living. Religion offers an external program or code of ethics that seeks to change outer behavior. That would be all right if that's where the problem is, but it's not. This sort of outer renovation usually blinds men to the real problem, which is the unreformable sin nature on the inside.

The good news of the "Gospel" is that God so loved the world that, at infinite cost to Himself, He provided a means of removing man's DEBT OF SIN and of dealing with the nature of sin in men. The Bible says that Jesus took our debt of sin and nailed it to His cross.

...the sound ... that saved a wretch like me! ...

...see. 'Twas grace that taught my heart to fear, ...

...ear. The hour I first believed. Through many ...

...ce hath brought me safe thus far. And grace will lead ...

...ord my hope secures. He will my shield and portion be ...

...shall fail, And mortal life shall cease. I shall po...

...shall soon dissolve like snow, The sun refuse to shine;

...mine. When we've been there ten thousand years,

...praise Than when we'd first begun. Amazing g...

...once was lost, but now am found; Was blind, bu...

...And grace my fears relieved; How precious did tha...

...any dangers, toils and snares, I have already come;

...ad me home. The Lord has promised good to me,

...be. As long as life endures Yea, when this flesh ...

...possess, within the veil, A life of joy and peace.

...e. But God, who called me here below, Shall be...

...Bright shining as the sun, We've no less days to ...

...grace! How sweet the sound That saved a wretch li...

...but now I see. 'Twas grace that taught...

Chapter
FIVE

BARRIER
NUMBER THREE:
SLAVERY TO SATAN

The first murder in history was committed because Cain was furious that God accepted Abel's offering and not his. Abel presented God with a blood sacrifice for his sin, which was given in obedience to God's previous instructions. Cain brought the work of His own hands, which was the first offering of religion. He was furious when God rejected that which depended on his own effort and merit. So, in a self-righteous rage he killed his brother. Religion hates competition, especially when it exposes man's lack of merit and acceptability to God.

When Adam believed Satan's lies about God

and disobeyed Him, he became the slave of Satan. All Adam's descendants are born under this same bondage unless a redemption is made to free them. When Jesus died for our sins, He paid the ransom price that broke Satan's legal right to hold us as slaves. This effectively dealt with this barrier and made it possible for each individual to choose to be set free.

Jesus is the only person ever born who was not born under Satan's dominion. The reason is that Jesus did not have a human father, and therefore the curse of SLAVERY TO SATAN didn't affect Him.

Satan's great worry is that when people find out that Jesus has paid the ransom for their freedom, they will see they no longer have to be Satan's slaves. This is why Satan works so hard to blind people to the Gospel of the grace of God.

Chapter
SIX

BARRIER
NUMBER FOUR:
SPIRITUAL DEATH

*A*dam and Eve had no idea how utterly disastrous it would be to be spiritually dead. When they sinned, they immediately felt an alienation from God and went so far as to hide from Him. These were the first observable indications that they had died spiritually. God had warned that *"in the day they ate of the tree of the knowledge of good and evil they would surely die."* They didn't die physically right then, but they instantly died spiritually. That part of their immaterial life that could know and communicate with God personally had died. In its place was a sense of alienation brought on by guilt.

Aside from all the other disastrous consequences of man's disobedience to God, perhaps the worst is that God withdrew from man His spiritual life and left man with a dead spirit, a spiritual vacuum if you please.

You can see the dilemma that arose between God and man. God made man in such a way that communication with him was possible through his spirit. So now God had to communicate with man in ways that his five senses could comprehend.

That's the whole story of the Bible—God seeking ways to make fallen man aware of His existence, His love, and His judgment against sin. But always God had to take the initiative and reach out to man in ways that he could understand by sight, hearing, taste, touch, or smell.

So here we have the complete picture of the universal barrier which separates man from God. Man can't tear the barrier down and he can't climb over it by his own efforts. In fact, he can't even climb over with God's help. The barrier must come down, and God alone can do that.

less days to sing God's praise ❧ Than when we'd first

ed a wretch like me! ❧ I once was lost, but now am fou

ght my heart to fear, ❧ And grace my fears relieved; ❧

ieved. ❧ Through many dangers, toils and snares, ❧

❧ And grace will lead me home. ❧ The Lord has p

ll my shield and portion be ❧ As long as life endures ❧

shall cease, ❧ I shall possess, within the veil, ❧ A li

The sun refuse to shine. ❧ But God, who called me

re ten thousand years, ❧ Bright shining as the sun. ❧

t begun. ❧ Amazing grace! How sweet the sound. ❧

found, ❧ Was blind, but now I see. ❧ 'Twas grace

Amaz... the sound ❧ That

'Twas grace that

believe

will

tal life

WHY GOD
HAD TO BECOME
A MAN

*M*arriage counselors tell us that the failure to communicate is one of the main factors in not being able to reconcile differences. Parents and children grow apart because of this problem.

The greatest breakdown in this area is between God and man. God has had to take into account man's inability to comprehend Him both as a person or a spiritual truth. He has been forced to reveal Himself to men in ways they could understand with their soulish life and their five senses.

God has spared no effort to reveal Himself

to man in terms of natural and material phenomena. The Spirit of God declared through David, *"The heavens are telling of the glory of God; and the firmament* [earth] *is declaring the work of His hands"* (Psalm 19:1).

This is one of the most profound things ever said in the Bible. It tells us that the great majesty and marvel of the universe—the beauty, the wonder, and the incredible balance of design and function—are the actual verbalization of the fact that there is an Almighty, Infinite God whose hands created them all.

The fact that day follows day with such certainty and night after night appears like clockwork is the same as God actually speaking to man about His reality and trustworthiness.

As powerful as God's nature lesson has been, it was never intended as God's ultimate revelation of Himself to man. The only way for God, who is a Spirit, to fully do and say what He wanted to, was to actually leave His eternal residence and enter the arena of humanity.

But what was the main necessity for God to come to earth?

It was to tear down the barriers man had erected between himself and God. No one but God was capable of doing that job. For a holy God who had an unquenchable love for man and a divine necessity to vindicate His justice, the only solution was to leave the glory of heaven, take on flesh and blood, and enter the human race.

Since it was human beings who had sinned and incurred the penalty of spiritual and physical death, another true human being would have to be God's final and permanent substitute for man. It would have to be someone of God's choosing who could qualify to step in as a substitute.

But in order for a man to qualify to take man's place of judgment and be his sin-bearer, there were five things that would have to be true of him: First, he would have to be a true human being, born into this world the same way other men are.

Second, he would have to be without any personal sin, either by inheritance or personal act.

Third, he would have to live under God's law and keep it perfectly.

Fourth, he would have to have full knowledge of what he was doing.

Fifth, he would have to be willing to take mankind's guilt as his own and be judged and put to death in the place of all mankind.

Such a man came into the world, according to specific predictions and promises, two thousand years ago. He perfectly fulfilled every qualification to be the Savior of men. That man was called Jesus of Nazareth, the Son of the Living God—both the Messiah to Israel and the Savior of all mankind.

Chapter EIGHT

THE MAN THAT GOD BECAME

*J*esus Christ who, as God, always existed in the Godhead with the Father and the Holy Spirit, some two thousand years ago left the Throne of God to come to earth and become a man.

Let's enumerate seven reasons why God found it necessary to take on visible form and become the man Jesus Christ.

First: God became a man in order to be the Savior of men. In writing about the origin of Jesus, the Apostle John calls Him a unique name, *"the Word."* He says the Word existed before the beginning of all things. He was there face to face with God and was, in fact, God. *"In the beginning was the Word, and the Word was with God, and the Word was God"* (John 1:1 NKJV). He was the personification of all the Father wanted to say.

Second: God became a man so that He could die for man's sin. The One who would take the penalty for man had to be a mortal human being as well as God. The writer of Hebrews makes this clear: *"But we see Jesus, who was made a little lower than the angels . . . that He, by the grace of God, might taste death for everyone"* (Hebrews 2:9 NKJV).

Third: God became a man to be a mediator. A mediator effects a reconciliation between estranged parties. Recall what Paul wrote to Timothy: *"For there is one God, and one mediator also between God and men, the man Christ Jesus"* (1 Timothy 2:5).

Fourth: God had to become a man to be our priest. Jesus is a high priest who's been in our shoes.

He knows what it's like to live under the pressures and temptations of this world. *"For we do not have a high priest who cannot sympathize with our weaknesses, but one who has been tempted in all things as we are, yet without sin. Let us therefore draw near with confidence to the throne of grace, that we may receive mercy and may find grace to help in time of need"* (Hebrews 4:15, 16).

Fifth: He became a man to be the revealer of God. Jesus said of Himself, *"He who has seen Me has seen the Father"* and *"I and the Father are one"* (John 14:9; 10:30). All that God wanted revealed of Himself, He revealed in the Person of His Son, Jesus.

Sixth: God became a man to occupy King David's throne. One of the great prophecies of the coming Messiah was that He would be a direct blood descendant of King David. Through Mary, the Messiah was given the blood right to the throne of David, because she was descended from the line of David's son Nathan. A curse was put upon the legal line from David's son Solomon. If Jesus had been the actual son of Joseph, who was from Solomon's line, He would have been under the curse. But by adoption, He got Joseph's legal right to David's throne without the blood curse.

Seventh: God had to become a man in order to be a "kinsman redeemer." Whenever a Jewish person was put into slavery, the only one who could pay the ransom price to release him was "nearest kinsman." In taking on humanity, Jesus became a "kinsman" of men and qualified to be the "kinsman redeemer."

Jesus was fully aware that He was God in the flesh. He boldly declared that:

- He came from God.

- He actually was God.

- He was to be worshiped.

- He could forgive people of their sins.

•He would rise from the dead.

•He would return to the Father to prepare a dwelling place for His children.

•He would one day return to earth to take us with Him into heaven.

Those declarations are too powerful to be ignored. We are faced with the question Jesus asked the disciples: *"Who do you say that I am?"* (Mark 8:29).

Millions of people will tell you, "I believe Jesus was a great moral teacher, but I don't accept His claim to be God." C. S. Lewis said of Jesus in *Mere Christianity:* "I'm trying here to prevent anyone saying the really foolish thing that people often say about Jesus: 'I'm ready to accept Jesus as a great moral teacher, but I don't accept His claim to be God.' That is the one thing we must not say. A man who was merely a man and said the sort of things Jesus said would not be a great moral teacher. He would either be a lunatic—on the level of the man who says he is

mazing grace! ... Was blind, but now I see. ... 'Twas grace that tau...
...cious did that grace appear ... The hour I first be...
...eady come; ... 'Tis grace hath brought me safe thus ...
...d to me, ... His Word my hope secures; ... He...
...en this flesh and heart shall fail, ... And mortal li...
...d peace. ... The world shall soon dissolve like snow,
...ow, ... Shall be forever mine. ... When we've been
...less days to sing God's praise ... Than when we'd
...ed a wretch like me! ... I once was lost, but now a...
...ight my heart to fear, ... And grace my fears relieve...
...ieved. ... Through many dangers, toils and snares,
... And grace will lead me home. ... The Lord
...f my shield and portion be ... As long as life endure...
...shall cease, ... I shall possess, within the veil, ...
...The sun refuse to shine; ... But God, who callea...
...re ten thousand years, ... Bright shining as the sun

a wretch ... I once was lost, but now am ...

... my heart to fear, And grace my fears relieved;

... Through many dangers, toils and snares,

... And grace will lead me home. The Lord

... will my shield and portion be, As long as life endu...

... shall cease, I shall possess, within the veil,

... The sun refuse to shine; But God, who call...

... here ten thousand years, Bright shining as the su...

... first begun. Amazing grace! How sweet the sou...

... found, Was blind, but now I see Twas

... How precious did that grace appear The

... I have already come, Tis grace hath brough...

... promised good to me, His Word my hope se...

... Yea, when this flesh and heart shall fail ...

... A life of joy and peace. The world shall soon dis...

... me here below, Shall be forever mine. Whe...

... We've no less days to sing God's praise ...

a poached egg—or else he would be the Devil of Hell. You must make your choice. Either this man was, and is, the Son of God, or else a madman or something worse. You can shut Him up for a fool, you can spit at Him and kill Him as a demon, or you can fall at His feet and call Him Lord and God. But let us not come up with any patronizing nonsense about His being just a great human teacher. He has not left that open to us. He did not intend to."[1]

There is only one conclusion: He is the promised Messiah, the Son of the living God.

1. C. S. Lewis, *Mere Christianity* (New York: The Macmillan Company, 1943).

PROPITIATION: WHY GOD AIN'T MADE ANYMORE

*'Twas grace that taught my heart to fear,
And grace my fears relieved;
How precious did that grace appear,
The hour I first believed.*

~CAPTAIN JOHN NEWTON

Why was it necessary for Christ to die on the cross? Was there no other possibility for God to reconcile men to Himself?

The most important reason for Christ's death on the cross is called "propitiation." The theological meaning of propitiation is to remove wrath by the satisfaction of offended righteousness and justice. Christ satisfied both of these offended attributes by fully paying our debt of sin. This removed them as a barrier to a relationship with man.

This act of propitiation removed God's wrath. As one southern brother put it, "God ain't mad anymore. He took all His anger out on Jesus."

Jesus was displayed publicly as a propitiation. God did this so the whole world would know His offended character had been "satisfied" by Jesus' death. God remains just in declaring righteous all who believe in His Son's substitutionary death.

This one act of Jesus has forever satisfied or propitiated God's justice and righteousness. The blood of Jesus is our guarantee that God will never again be angry with anyone who believes in Jesus as his personal Savior. Jesus' blood turned God's throne from one of judgment to one of mercy.

Chapter TEN

REDEMPTION: NO LONGER SLAVES

*L*isten to the powerful way Paul convinces his hearers that they have been set free from their sinful indebtedness to God: *"And when you were dead in your transgressions and the uncircumcision of your flesh, He made you alive together with Him, having forgiven us all our transgressions, having canceled out the certificate of debt consisting of decrees against us and which was hostile to us; and He has taken it out of the way, having nailed it to the cross"* (Colossians 2:13, 14).

Paul gives a picture of Jesus taking our

certificate of debt and nailing it to His cross. In doing this, it was saying He made Himself guilty for every sin listed on every human being's certificate of debt.

Do you know why He did it?

So you and I would never have to be alone again. So He can now promise those who believe in Him, *"I will never desert you, nor will I ever forsake you"* (Hebrews 13:5).

But that's not the end of the story.

Just before Jesus gave up His earthly life and commended His Spirit to the Father, He shouted a word which is the Magna Carta of freedom for all true believers. That victorious cry was the Greek word *telelestai.* Let that word burn like a firebrand into your mind. That's the word a Roman judge would write across a released criminal's certificate of debt to show that all his penalty had been paid and he was free at last. It is translated in John 19:30 as "It is finished," but should be "Paid in Full."

In the mind of God, "Paid in Full" has been written with the blood of Jesus Christ across the certificate of debt of every man who will ever live. Christ has redeemed all mankind from Satan's slave market of sin. Unfortunately, not everyone has chosen to accept the ransom and go free.

The story is told of a young man who was convicted of murder many years ago. His parents, being influential and wealthy, finally obtained a stay of execution, and eventually the convict was pardoned. This man, sitting on death row, was given the news that he had his freedom. But when he was handed the pardon, he rejected it. He said, "I'm guilty and I want to die."

His family and lawyers couldn't persuade him to change his mind. In an effort to keep him from being executed, the family took the case all the way to the highest court in the state. The court ruled that a pardon is not a pardon until it is accepted by the one for whom it was intended. The man went to his death because he refused to accept the pardon.

So it is with men. Those who spend eternity separated from God will do so, not because there isn't an alternative, but because they won't accept the pardon that already has their name on it.

Once a man accepts the pardon, he's forever free. Not just after he dies, either. He's free in this life, in the here-and-now as well as the sweet-by-and-by.

If you've never done so before, why not take this moment to thank Jesus Christ for dying for you and accept His gracious pardon and forgiveness. You'll be eternally glad you did!

Chapter ELEVEN

SUBSTITUTIONARY DEATH

*B*illy Graham was driving through a small town in the South and was picked up by radar in a speed trap. He was clocked over the speed limit. A squad car pulled him over and a police officer instructed him to follow the car to the local justice of the peace. The justice was a barber, and his office was in the barber shop.

Graham walked into the place and the justice was shaving a man. Finishing the job, he turned to Graham and reviewed his case. "How do you plead?" the justice asked.

"Guilty, your honor," Graham said.

"That'll be $15," replied the justice.

Graham reached for his wallet to pay the fine.

The justice shot him a second glance and said, "Say, aren't you Billy Graham, the evangelist?"

"I regret to say, sir, that I am," Graham responded, hopefully tucking the wallet back into his pocket.

"That'll be $15," the man said again with a smile. "But I'll tell you what I'm going to do," said the justice after a moment's hesitation. "I'm going to pay the fine for you."

He reached for his billfold, took out a five- and a ten-dollar bill, slipped them in the till, and closed the drawer.

"You've been a big help to me and my family, and this is something I want to do," he said.

The law had been broken, the penalty assessed, and the fine had to be paid. But in this case, as in the case of God versus mankind, a substitute came forward and volunteered to pay the fine. It didn't cost Billy Graham's "savior" much to pay Billy's fine, but the cost to God to provide a savior to pay our "fine" of death was the death of His Son.

When Jesus was hanging on the cross as our substitute, the writer tells us it was that *"He, by the grace of God, might taste death for everyone"* (Hebrews 2:9 NKJV). Since man's penalty for being a sinner is both spiritual and physical death, Jesus had to taste both kinds of death.

In dying spiritually and physically as our substitute, God looked at Jesus' death and credited it to the account of the fallen race. His spiritual death means God can give spiritual life to all men who will receive it, and His physical death—and the defeat of His physical death by the resurrection—set God free to justly raise our physical bodies and give them immortality. This is grace heaped upon grace.

The only question is, "Why did He do it?" Jesus gave us the answer when He told His disciples, *"Greater love has no one than this, that one lay down his life for his friends"* (John 15:13). Jesus died for us because He loved us!

mazing grace! How sweet the sound ☙ That saved a

Was blind, but now I see. ☙ Twas grace that taught n

cious did that grace appear ☙ The hour I first believed

eady come; ☙ Tis grace hath brought me safe thus far,

d to me. ☙ His Word my hope secures; ☙ He will

en this flesh and heart shall fail, ☙ And mortal life sha

d peace. ☙ The world shall soon dissolve like snow,

ow, ☙ Shall be forever mine. ☙ When we've been there

less days to sing God's praise ☙ Than when we'd first

ed a wretch like me! ☙ I once was lost, but now am fou

ght my heart to fear, ☙ And grace my fears relieved;

ieved. ☙ Through many dangers, toils and snares,

, ☙ And grace will lead me home. ☙ The Lord has

l my shield and portion be, ☙ As long as life endures

shall cease, ☙ I shall possess, within the veil. ☙ A li

The sun refuse to shine; ☙ But God, who called me

re ten thousand years, ☙ Bright shining as the sun,

st begun. ☙ Amazing grace! How sweet the sound ☙

found. ☙ Was blind, but now I see. ☙ Twas

TWELVE

RECONCILIATION

To me one of the happiest words in the English language is "reconciliation." It's one of God's favorite words, too, because it means He can now restore man to fellowship with Himself because of Christ's work on the cross. Reconciliation means God isn't angry with us anymore, and He no longer holds our sins against us.

The Lord Jesus bore all the anger God had against my sins and against me, the sinner. When I found out that God wasn't angry with me anymore, I stopped running from Him and turned to Him. This is called reconciliation.

True reconciliation always does away with hostility or fear. If we feel our sins are still an issue between us and God, then we don't feel like going to Him. But listen to this good news from the Apostle Paul: *"God was in Christ reconciling the world to Himself, not counting their trespasses against them, and He has committed to us the word of reconciliation"* (2 Corinthians 5:19).

Did you get it? God isn't holding our sins against us anymore.

A beautiful illustration of reconciliation is the parable Jesus told about the prodigal son (Luke 15). He was trying to show it's better to admit you're a sinner and place yourself under God's grace than to bravely defend your self-righteousness and miss out on God's grace.

In the parable there was a father with two sons. The younger one decided he wanted his inheritance so he could leave home and live it up (he represents sinners). The older son (he represents self-righteousness) stayed at home and continued to work for his father (he represents God).

The younger son went to a far-off country and squandered his inheritance with wild living. A famine came, and he was in real need. So he hired out to a certain citizen and found himself out in the fields feeding pigs.

Finally the boy said to himself, "This is ridiculous! I'm here starving while my father's slaves have better food than this. I will go to my father and tell him, 'Father, I know I've sinned against heaven and you by the stupid way I've blown my inheritance, and I'm not even worthy to be a son of yours. But if you'll let me come home, I'll be glad just to be one of your servants.' "

He expected his father to have nothing to do with him after the way he'd disappointed him. But he was in for a big surprise! While he was still a long way from his father's house, his dad caught sight of him. The father must have been keeping an eye out for him. When he saw him, he ran to his son and threw his arms around him and kissed him.

The boy began the speech, but his father never heard a word he said. He was already giving instructions to the servants to get a big welcome-home party ready. There was no resentment or wrath in the father toward that boy even though there was plenty of reason for him to be upset.

The father's attitude was expressed in his statement, *"This son of mine was dead and has come to life again; he was lost, and has been found"* (Luke 15:24).

RECONCILIATION ISN'T REASONABLE

This parable is a terrific illustration of reconciliation. During all those long months and possibly years, the father kept on loving the boy and yearning for him to come home and be reconciled to him. The boy expected there to be stern barriers between him and his father. But when he returned to his dad, he found that instead of barriers there was love and complete acceptance. The fact that the father said of his son that he was *"dead and has come to life again; he was lost and has been found"* shows a radical change had taken place in their relationship. That change is called reconciliation.

Reconciliation is worth nothing unless the barriers that caused it are torn down and then the one who is alienated decides to become reconciled. The prodigal son had to decide to go home. That's simply called "repenting," which means to "change your mind and your direction."

God has made all men "reconcilable."

of a wretch like m... I once was lost, but now am foun...

ght my heart to fea... And grace my fears relieved;

ieved. Through many dangers, toils and snares,

ar, And grace will lead me home. The Lord has

will my shield and portion be, As long as life endures

shall cease, I shall possess, within the veil, A li...

The sun refuse to shine; But God, who called m...

here ten thousand years, Bright shining as the sun,

irst begun . Amazing grace! How sweet the sound

found; Was blind, but now I see. Twas grac...

How precious did that grace appear The hour

Tis grace hath brought me

Word my hope secures;

And

Chapter

THIRTEEN

THE DECISION
OF DESTINY

od so loved the "world" that He gave His
Son (John 3:16). Christ didn't die for just
part of the world, but for the whole world. It was for
those who would ridicule His name, ignore His salvation, despise His Word, and reject His authority.

The whole world has been made "savable"
because of the death of Christ on the cross. But being
"savable" and being "saved" are two different things.
If someone puts $1 million in a bank account for you,
it won't do any good unless, first, you know about it
and, second, you draw upon it.

I once heard a speaker liken God's worldwide
offer of salvation to a pet store owner who puts a free

kitten in the window of is shop. It's available to everyone, but it only becomes the possession of the one who goes in and claims it. God has put His offer of "free forgiveness" in His window, and it's available to everyone but only the possession of those who come in and take it.

We keep running into a word in the New Testament that tells us the basis on which God accepts us. That word is GRACE. If we could have only a half-dozen words in our vocabulary, that word should be one of them. It's loaded with meaning. Simply put, grace means to freely give something to someone which he can in no possible way deserve, merit, or earn.

The instant there's a hint of someone trying to earn what's being given, then it is no longer given by grace. *"And if by grace, then it is no longer by works; if it were, grace would no longer be grace"* (Romans 11:6 NIV).

What is it that God has given that we can't in any way merit? His righteousness, love, forgiveness, acceptance, mercy, redemption, inheritance, and eternal life—all of which are wrapped up in one package called "salvation." It's given completely on the basis of "grace."

If you had a present for a loved one and he kept trying to do something to earn it, you'd feel rebuffed. If you wanted him to work for the present, then it wouldn't really be a gift; it would be a wage. That's what Paul says about man's efforts to work for God's favor: *"Now when a man works, his wages are not credited to him as a gift, but as an obligation. However, to the man who does not work but trusts God who justifies the wicked, his faith is credited as righteousness"* (Romans 4:4, 5 NIV).

It is a very serious matter to make expensive that which cost God the death of His beloved Son to make free.

The Apostle Paul taught what is necessary to be saved: *"If you confess with your mouth Jesus as Lord, and believe in your heart that God raised Him from the dead, you shall be saved; for with the heart man believes, resulting in righteousness, and with the mouth he confesses, resulting in salvation"* (Romans 10:9, 10).

Any ritual, be it circumcision, communion, or baptism, when it is added to faith as a condition of salvation, it becomes a work of human merit. And that is totally incompatible with grace. God has always had only one way of saving men, and that's been on the basis of *"grace . . . through faith . . . not as a result of works, that no one should boast"* (Ephesians 2:8, 9).

Remember the thief on the cross beside Jesus. He believed in Christ while nailed to a cross. He couldn't come down from the cross and do any good deeds, he couldn't be baptized, and he couldn't go out and manifest the Christian life to the world by holy living. Nevertheless, Jesus told him that before the day ended he would be in paradise with Him because he had believed on Jesus. If God could save a thief by faith alone—and He did—then He must do it the same way for everyone.

I said at the beginning of this chapter that if someone deposited $1 million in a bank account for you, it would be of no benefit to you unless you knew about it and then withdrew it from the bank. Now you know what it is that God has done for you on the cross and how to draw upon it by faith alone.

...That saved a wretch like me! ... I once was lost, b...

grace that taught my heart to fear, ... And grace my fea...

...have believed. ... Through many dangers, toils a...

...me safe thus far, ... And grace will lead me home. ...

...cases; ... He will my shield and portion be, ... As long

And mortal life shall cease, ... I shall possess, within th...

...white like snow, ... The sun refuse to shine; ... But Go...

...hen we've been there ten thousand years, ... Bright shini...

...han when we'd first begun. ... Amazing grace! How su...

lost, but now am found; ... Was blind, but now I see.

...my fears relieved; ... How precious did that grace appear...

...ils and snares, ... I have already come; ... Tis grace h...

... The Lord has promised good to me, ... His Word...

...g as life endures ... Yea, when this flesh and heart shal...

...n the veil, ... A life of joy and peace. ... The world sho...

God, who call'd me here below; ... Shall be forever mine.

...ning as the sun, ... We've no less days to sing God's pra...

...sweet the sound ... That saved a wretch like...

Chapter
FOURTEEN

JUSTIFICATION

A simple definition for "justification" is "just-as-if-I'd-never-sinned." It makes a clever-sounding phrase, but unfortunately it only explains the negative half of justification.

Christ has taken my sins away, but even having no sin will never make me acceptable in God's eyes. To be acceptable to God, I need more than the subtraction of my sins. I need the addition of Christ's righteousness.

Paul tells us how God arranged for this exchange. God made Christ *"who knew no sin to be sin on our behalf, that we might become the righteousness of God in Him"* (2 Corinthians 5:21). In other words, God took our sins and put them on Christ and then took Christ's righteousness and gave it to us in exchange.

That's what it means to be justified. God is now free to instantly and irrevocably "declare righteous" any man, woman, or child who places faith in Christ as Savior. God declares that person to be just as righteous in His sight as His Son, Jesus Christ. This is our new "standing" with God.

God sees me through the grid of Jesus' righteousness, and therefore I am as acceptable to Him as His Son Jesus is, regardless of my daily performance. Righteousness is given to a person, free and complete, the moment he places faith in Christ as Savior. It cannot be improved upon, added to, nor ever revoked.

God assures us He would not revoke our justification. *"What, then, shall we say in response to this? If God is for us, who can be against us? He who did not spare his own Son, but gave him up for us all—how will he not also, along with him, graciously give us all things? Who will bring any charge against those whom God has chosen? It is God who justifies"* (Romans 8:31-33 NIV).

If we think our relationship with God is in constant jeopardy because of our failure to live the Christian life correctly, then we will be a nervous wreck. I can never experience peace with God until I begin to count as true the fact that I have been given Christ's righteousness and my eternal relationship with God is secure. If God says He is at peace with us on the basis of our justification, then what right do we have not to be at peace with God?

A STANDING IN AMAZING GRACE

God cannot deal with us in any other way than grace. It's so hard for people to really believe this. Most can accept the fact that they could do nothing to deserve or earn their initial salvation, but most Christians have the idea that they must earn the right to be used by God or receive His blessings after becoming His child.

When did any of us ever deserve anything from a holy and righteous God except His wrath? Yet, God gives us His gracious blessings at any time, quite apart from any merit in us. It's because of our standing in grace with Him.

One of the marvelous things about being in an atmosphere of grace is that you don't have to walk around on eggshells worrying about offending someone. We are standing in grace with Him, and He doesn't get bugged with us when we fail. You see, our acceptance with Him is based on one key factor only: we are in His Son and His Son's righteousness is in us. Paul wrote, *"There is therefore now no condemnation for those who are in Christ Jesus"* (Romans 8:1).

I remember the day that truth hit me! I was so under a pile of self-condemnation, and what I thought was God's condemnation, that I could hardly see out from under the pile. I was reading that verse and realized I wasn't under God's condemnation now and never could be again. That set the stage for me to stop condemning myself and stop believing others who tried to make me feel guilty because I wasn't living up to their ideas of what a Christian ought to be.

In Romans 8 Paul joyously writes, *"If God be for us, who can be against us?"* (verse 31 KJV). This is no longer a defeated and despairing believer. He realized there was no more condemnation from the Law, from God, and consequently no legitimate condemnation from his own conscience, because he was in Christ Jesus. Realizing that he didn't have to live for God in order not to be condemned, Paul began to relax and trust the Holy Spirit to live the Christian life through him.

GOD IS ON OUR SIDE

God promised to freely give us thousands of privileges and blessings outlined in the Bible. There's no need to beg at the back door of heaven for your needs. Paul wrote, *"My God shall supply all your needs according to His riches in glory in Christ Jesus"* (Philippians 4:19).

When we go to the Lord in prayer and repentance, we find a gracious and loving acceptance no matter how we have been behaving in our Christian lives.

Since God has gone to great lengths to prove He doesn't condemn us, then do we have a right to condemn ourselves? No one can have a bold faith when he's condemning himself for his miserable performance as a child of God.

True faith comes from focusing on Christ and what He's done for you. But if you don't concentrate on that and instead focus on your behavior, you'll soon end up being discouraged and condemning yourself for your failure to live up to what God requires.

It's also true that if you condemn yourself for a shabby Christian life, you're bound to also have a critical view of others. We hate most in others what we hate about ourselves. Yet if Christ doesn't condemn a brother but accepts and declares him righteous in Christ, then what right do I have to condemn him?

Nobody wants to snuggle up to a porcupine, and if an erring believer thinks God is still angry with him and just waiting to condemn him, he'll never come back to the Lord. Our loving and accepting attitude may be his path back to fellowship with God and the Church.

That's AMAZING GRACE!

And mortal life shall cease, ☙ I shall possess, within

dissolve like snow, ☙ The sun refuse to shine; ☙ But

When we've been there ten thousand years, ☙ Bright shin

Than when we'd first begun. ☙ Amazing grace! How

s lost, but now am found, ☙ Was blind, but now I se

e my fears relieved. ☙ How precious did that grace appe

toils and snares ☙ I have already come ☙ 'Tis grace

☙ The Lord has promised good to me ☙ His Wo

long as I endures ☙ Yea, when this flesh and heart sh

thin the veil, ☙ A life of joy and peace ☙ The world

God, who called me here below, ☙ Shall be forever min

shining as the sun, ☙ We've no less days to sing God's

w sweet the sound ☙ That saved a wretch like me! ☙

I see. ☙ 'Twas grace that taught my heart to fear, ☙ E

ow saved the wretch ☙ That saved a wretch like me! ☙

I see. ☙ 'Twas grace that taught my heart to fear, ☙

e appear ☙ The hour I first believed. ☙ Through m

is grace hath brought me safe thus far, ☙ And grace wil

FORGIVENESS

*T*n Colossians Paul sets forth the extent of God's forgiveness. He speaks to the young believers in the church at Colossae: *"And when you were dead in your transgressions* [sins] *and the uncircumcision of your flesh, He made you alive together with Him, having forgiven us all our* [sins]*"* (Colossians 2:13).

I want to lock in on one particular phrase in this verse, "forgiven us all our sins." Have you ever stopped to consider how much "all" really is? A lawyer told me about a legal decision from a case in Pennsylvania. The word "all" was defined this way: "All includes everything and excludes nothing."

In the mind of the average Christian, when he reads the words *"having forgiven us all our sins,"* he thinks it refers to all the sins he committed before he accepted Jesus. I used to think this.

Okay—born 1929, received Christ 1955. I used to think that when I believed in Jesus Christ as my personal Savior, He forgave me all my sins from the day I was born up until 1955 on the basis of His death in A.D. 33. I don't know what I thought His provision was for the rest of my life!

How many of my sins were future when Christ died? ALL OF THEM! They were so offensive to God that in A.D. 33 He dealt with everything I would ever do wrong. My future sins were as real and repugnant to God as my past ones.

By Christ's sacrifice, He has provided a forgiveness for us that's eternal and irreversible. Isaiah the prophet quoted the Lord as saying, *"I, even I, am the one who wipes out your transgressions for My own sake; and I will not remember your sins"* (Isaiah 43:25).

Two truths form the bedrock foundation upon which you must build to experience the reality of God's forgiveness in your daily life. First, all your sins—past, present, and future—were forgiven when you believed in Jesus. There are none He hasn't already forgiven. Second, not only has He forgiven you all your sins, but He's wiped them out from His own memory forever. They'll never be brought up against you again.

CAN WE FORGIVE AS GOD HAS?

If God has forgiven us all our sins and isn't holding them against us anymore, then what should our attitude be about sins in ourselves and others?

There are many people who have never been able to forgive themselves for their past sins. Maybe they've had a secret habit which they've felt was sin, and because they can't forgive themselves, they develop a sense of shame that results in a terrible self-image.

Or, a knowledge of their inner sin life causes some people to develop a defensiveness that makes them hostile and argumentative. They're going to be very sure no one gets close enough to see how raunchy they are inside.

Was blind, but now I see. 'Twas grace that taught

...cious did that grace appear. The hour I first believe...

...ady come. 'Tis grace hath brought me safe thus far

...d to me. His Word my hope secures, He wi...

...en this flesh and heart shall fail, And mortal life...

...t peace. The world shall soon dissolve like snow.

...w. Shall be forever mine. When we've been the...

...less days singing God's praise. Then when we'd fir...

...et a wretch like me! I once was lost, but now am...

...the fear. How grace my fears relieved...

...through many dangers, toils and snares,...

...grace will lead me home. The Lord ha...

...shield and portion be, as long as life endures...

...For all... within the veil.

...God who called...

...ousand years...

my heart to fear, & And grace my fears relieved; &

d. & Through many dangers, toils and snares, & E

& And grace will lead me home. & The Lord has

my shield and portion be, & As long as life endures

al cease, & I shall possess, within the veil, & A lif

The sun refuse to shine; & But God, who called me

ten thousand years & Bright shining as the sun, &

begun. & Amazing grace! How sweet the sound &

re. & Was blind, but now I see. & 'Twas grace

& How precious did that grace appear & The hour

I have already come; & 'Tis grace hath brought me

promised good to me. & His Word my hope secures,

& Yea, when this flesh and heart shall fail, & And

life of joy and peace. & The earth shall soon dissolve

here below, & Shall be

There's only one basis on which we can forgive ourselves and others. We must remember and believe that God has already forgiven us for the sins that are causing the bitterness. If God has forgiven us and is not holding our sins against us, then we should not hold them against ourselves.

For me to fail to forgive myself or anyone else who has offended me is to say that I have a higher standard of forgiveness than God. God already has forgiven whatever it is I can't forgive. He forgave me things that are infinitely more hurtful than what any mere human can do to me.

When I knowingly sin, it breaks FELLOWSHIP WITH GOD, NOT MY ETERNAL RELATIONSHIP. I must confess my sin to the Lord, according to I John 1:9: *"If we confess our sins, He is faithful and just to forgive us our sins and to cleanse us from all unrighteousness"* (NKJV). I must agree verbally with God about my known sins.

God says He has forgiven all my sins, including this one I just committed. So I look to the cross of

Jesus and thank Him that in His sight my sin has already been forgiven. Out of appreciation for such grace in forgiveness, I accept it gratefully, turn from my sin, and begin to focus consciously upon the Lord Jesus.

After I have confessed a sin, Satan will attempt to accuse my conscience and make me believe that I am really not forgiven. He will cause me to feel, "God won't forgive me this time." This sort of thinking is an insult to God's grace.

There's no longer any reason to focus on past sins. The work of Christ has completely dealt with our sins. They can never again be brought up against us.

I can't find a verse of Scripture that teaches a believer to avoid sins by "worrying about them." Forgive yourself for what you've held in your conscience. Forgive those toward whom you've been harboring bitterness and unforgiveness. *"And be kind to one another, tender-hearted, forgiving each other, just as God in Christ also has forgiven you"* (Ephesians 4:32).

This is the pathway to freedom!

Amazing grace! How sweet the sound ❧ That saved a

Was blind, but now I see. ❧ 'Twas grace that taught

ecious did that grace appear ❧ The hour I first believed

ready come; ❧ 'Tis grace hath brought me safe thus far,

od to me, ❧ His Word my hope secures; ❧ He will

hen this flesh and heart shall fail, ❧ And mortal life sha

d peace. ❧ The world shall soon dissolve like snow, ❧

low, ❧ Shall be forever mine. ❧ When we've been there

less days to sing God's praise ❧ Than when we'd first

ved a wretch like me! ❧ I once was lost, but now am fo

ught my heart to fear, ❧ And grace my fears relieved; ❧

lieved. ❧ Through many dangers, toils and snares, ❧

, ❧ And grace will lead me home. ❧ The Lord has

ll my shield and portion be, ❧ As long as life endures

e shall cease, ❧ I shall possess, within the veil, ❧ A

The sun refuse to shine, ❧ But God, who called me

e ten thousand years, ❧ Bright shining as the sun, ❧

t begun. ❧ Amazing grace! How sweet the sound ❧

SIXTEEN

FREEDOM

When we've been there ten thousand years,
Bright shining as the sun,
We've no less days to sing God's praise,
Than when we'd first begun.

~CAPTAIN JOHN NEWTON

*I*f there's one word that expresses the yearning of mankind today, it is FREEDOM. In every language created by man, "freedom" is a word that is cherished. Regardless of what a person owns, they would rather lose their possessions than their freedom.

You don't have to have irons around your legs to be a slave. The crowd to whom Jesus said, *"If therefore the Son shall make you free, you shall be free indeed"* (John 8:36), were not standing in shackles. Jesus explained their bondage was an inner one. They belonged to Satan.

There are two aspects to the freedom which the redemptive work of Christ has made available. First, we've been set free from the penalty of sin by the death of Christ for us. That took care of removing the barriers that separated us from a holy and righteous God. But second, His death also has provided for a daily deliverance of believers from the power of sin. To make this possible, Christ died, not only for sins, but for the sinner himself. This made it possible for the Holy Spirit to take up permanent residence in every believer.

Paul tells us this is the reason we can now *"consider ourselves to be dead to* [the sin nature], *but alive to God in Christ Jesus"* (Romans 6:11).

One of Satan's favorite tactics to keep believers enslaved is to get them to try to live for God by keeping all His laws. But, Christ's resurrection proved to be Satan's final undoing. When Jesus rose from the dead, He disarmed the rulers and authorities—referring to Satan and demons—and made a public spectacle of them in showing His triumph over them.

There's a critical truth here. Since we were crucified and raised with Christ, His victory over Satan and demons is our victory, too. Their legal right to touch us is forever gone.

A clear illustration of this truth is the story that follows. It's a case on record from many years back.

A ship at sea had a captain so ruthless and brutal to his men that they became desperate and fearful for their safety.

In maritime law, the captain of a ship is the absolute master until officially relieved from command by the country of the ship's registry.

The first mate aboard the vessel was an understanding and humanly sympathetic man, respected by all hands. After much personal consideration and real insistence on the part of the entire crew, he radioed the home port, reporting the atrocities of the captain against his men, and requested permission to assume command at once.

A message was flashed back commissioning him to take official command. The former captain was to be relieved of all authority effective immediately. He was to be held aboard ship and brought home to stand trial. He was allowed freedom to move about on deck, but it was made clear to the entire crew that he had been relieved of his command.

Before long the former captain decided to test his power. A seaman was busy at work, enjoying the leadership of the new captain. The old captain came by, jerked the man up, and began issuing stern orders. The seaman was so accustomed to following his commands that he instinctively obeyed. And as soon as he started to obey, the old captain proceeded to lay it on all the more.

Amidst the verbal barrage, the seaman realized the man had no authority over him. He began to resist—and got the beating of his life. Bruised and battered, he told his rightful commander of the incident.

The new captain told him that if the former commander tried this again, to call him and he would take care of the old captain.

Let's face it. We're at war. But God wants us to know that we no longer have to give in to the demands of our sin natures. We are no longer under the law, and we have been liberated from Satan's authority and dominion. The ransom was paid by Jesus, and we've been set free. The only slavery for us now is our willing slavery to Jesus out of love and gratitude.

God doesn't demand that we become His servants, but Paul says it's the only reasonable thing to do in light of all God has done for us. *"But now having been set free from sin, and having become slaves of God, you have your fruit to holiness, and the end, everlasting life"* (Romans 6:22 NKJV).

That saved a wretch like me! ❧ I once was lost, but no

e that taught my heart to fear, ❧ And grace my fears re

I first believed. ❧ Through many dangers, toils and s

safe thus far, ❧ And grace will lead me home. ❧ Th

❧ He will my shield and portion be, ❧ As long as li

mortal life shall cease, ❧ I shall possess, within the veil

like snow, ❧ The sun refuse to shine; ❧ But God, wh

we've been there ten thousand years, ❧ Bright shining as

when we'd first begun. ❧ Amazing grace! How sweet t

but now am found, ❧ Was blind, but now I see. ❧

are relieved. ❧ How precious did that grace appear ❧

❧ have already come, ❧

Lord my

when my

shall fail,

shall see

REGENERATION: A NEW BIRTH

You have made us for Yourself, O God,
And our hearts are restless
Until they find their rest in You.

~AUGUSTINE

Every spring plants emerge from their wintry slumber and sprout forth fresh, green vegetation. It is fascinating to put a kernel of corn into the ground and to see new life spring forth from it.

Yet there is a far greater miracle—the regeneration of the human spirit made possible through Christ's death on the cross. The moment we place our trust in Christ's death we're reborn spiritually.

All mankind is born physically alive but spiritually dead. That part of us that had the same kind of life as God died in the original sin of Adam. When we believe in Jesus as our sin-bearer, we are miraculously born spiritually. This new spirit enables us for the first time to know God on a personal basis. Indeed, the light of divine life begins to shine into our darkness.

One of the clearest declarations of man's need to be born again is a conversation Jesus had with Israel's leading religious teacher, Nicodemus. In this conversation Jesus revealed that man must have a new spiritual birth before he can understand the truth about God and His kingdom.

"Now there was a man of the Pharisees, named Nicodemus, a ruler of the Jews; this man came to Him [Jesus] *by night, and said to Him, 'Rabbi, we know that You have come from God as a teacher; for no one can do these signs that You do unless God is with him.'*

"Jesus answered and said to him, 'Truly, truly, I say to you, unless one is born again [from above], he cannot see the kingdom of God.'

"Nicodemus said to Him, 'How can a man be born when he is old? He cannot enter a second time into his mother's womb and be born, can he?'

"Jesus answered, 'Truly, truly, I say to you, unless one is born of water and the Spirit, he cannot enter into the kingdom of God. That which is born of the flesh is flesh; and that which is born of the Spirit is spirit.

" 'Do not marvel that I said to you, "You must be born again."

" 'The wind blows where it wishes and you hear the sound of it, but do not know where it comes from and where it is going; so is every one who is born of the Spirit' " (John 3:1-8).

The great French philosopher and theologian, Pascal, called man's spiritual void a "God-shaped vacuum which only Christ could fill." This vacuum plays an important role. It serves as a reminder that something is missing. Augustine described it this way: "You have made us for Yourself, O God, and our hearts are restless until they find their rest in You."

Until the One who made us comes to dwell in His rightful place in our spirits, we will never feel complete. There will always be something missing. This accounts for why people pursue sex, money, fame, power, position, beauty, pleasure, religion, and even the occult. Even the "do gooders" without Christ are simply trying to fill their sense of an inner vacuum.

The Bible pictures the unregenerate man as "walking in darkness." That is why he tries to substitute things for Jesus. When Adam sinned, spiritual darkness filled the vacuum left by his dead spirit. His spiritual light was gone. God's plan was to restore His light to this darkened void.

The greatest authority on the subject of "light" was Jesus. He called Himself *the light of the world; He who follows Me shall not walk in the darkness, but shall have the light of life"* (John 8:12).

When a person is born again, the light really goes on inside him. For the first time he's able to understand the things of God and perceive the spiritual realm. And God begins to shine that new light onto his path and show him His will.

It's because we've been given this inner light that Paul admonishes us the way he does in Ephesians 5:1-8. He talks about a number of sins that unregenerate men freely participate in: greed, immorality, silly and dirty talk, coveting, and so forth. Then he says, *"Do not be partakers with them, for you were formerly darkness, but now you are light in the Lord; walk as children of light"* (verses 7, 8).

That's a terrific description of born-again believers—*"children of light."* If there's anything this dark old world needs, it's light. The only true source of light is the *"children of light."* That's why Jesus said,

"Let your light shine before men in such a way that they may see your good works, and glorify your Father who is in heaven" (Matthew 5:16).

Faith is the eyesight of this new spiritual nature. It enables us to reach out to God and to know Him. Faith enables us to believe when God says He will do something, He absolutely will.

The best way to understand faith is this: It is our response to God's ability to cope with our problems through us. If I believe He's able, then I'll automatically have faith. If I don't know how trustworthy He is, then no amount of spiritual gimmickry is going to make me trust Him.

Jesus said, *"I tell you the truth, if you have faith as small as a mustard seed, you can say to this mountain, 'Move from here to there' and it will move. Nothing will be impossible for you"* (Matthew 17:20 NIV).

You can have 20/20 vision and yet look at a mountain fifty miles away and not see it very clearly.

What's the problem? You don't need better eyesight; you need to get closer to the mountain. That's the way faith works. We are all given 20/20 faith when we're born again. But faith needs an object in order for it to function, and God is the object.

If Jesus has not seemed as real to you as you want, and you've felt that you needed more faith to bring Him closer, then what you really need is to get a closer view of this wonderful Object. You do this by getting into His Word. His promises will become believable. Technically your faith does not grow, but your concept of Jesus does. The end result will be a new certainty of God. You will find yourself loving and responding to Him in a way you never thought possible.

One of my favorite songs has the first line, "I believe in miracles, I've seen a soul set free." To me, the greatest miracle is God's salvation work of undoing the internal damage to man's spirit, soul, and body and bringing back the original harmony and balance.

mazing grace! How sweet the sound That saved

Was blind, but now I see. Twas grace that taugh

cious did that grace appear The hour I first belie

eady come; Tis grace hath brought me safe thus fa

d to me, His Word my hope secures; He w

en this flesh and heart shall fail, And mortal life

t peace. The world shall soon dissolve like snow,

ow, Shall be forever mine. When we've been th

less days to sing God's praise Than when we'd fir

ed a wretch like me! I once was lost, but now am

ght my heart to fear, And grace my fears relieved;

ieved. Through many dangers, toils and snares

, And grace will lead me home The Lord ha

l my shield and portion be, As long as life endures

shall cease, I shall possess, within the veil

The sun refuse to shine; But God, who called

re ten thousand years Bright shining as the sun,

t beauty, Amazing grace! How sweet the sound

wretch like me! ☙ I once was lost, but now am foun

my heart to fear, ☙ And grace my fears relieved,

d. ☙ Through many dangers, toils and snares, ☙

☙ And grace will lead me home. ☙ The Lord has

my shield and portion be, ☙ As long as life endures

all cease, ☙ I shall possess, within the veil, ☙ A li

The sun refuse to shine; ☙ But God, who called me

e ten thousand years, ☙ Bright shining as the sun,

begun. ☙ Amazing grace! How sweet the sound

und. ☙ Was blind, but now I see. ☙ 'Twas grace

☙ How precious did that grace appear, ☙ The hour

I have already come, ☙ 'Tis grace hath brought me

promised good to me, ☙ His blood my soul secures

Yea, when this flesh and heart shall fail, ☙ And

fe of joy and peace. ☙ The world shall soon dissolve

here below, ☙ Shall be forever mine. ☙ When we

We've no less days to sing God's praise ☙ Than

That saved a wretch like me! ☙ I once was lost

Paul amplifies this when he says, *"Therefore if any man is in Christ, he is a new creature; the old things passed away; behold, new things have come"* (2 Corinthians 5:17).

What were those old things that passed away?

Basically, your "Old Man" passed away. That's everything you were in Adam—spiritually dead, hostile to God, under the Law, headed for eternity in hell, a slave of Satan, dominated by your soulish life and the flesh, and unrighteous and self-centered.

God declares the old things passed away when we were born again and that all things became new. This is already true by a divine fiat. What God declares in His Word to be true of me is the most true thing there is, whether I feel it or not.

Regeneration created our new spiritual life the moment we believed in Christ. But the repercussions progressively take place throughout our whole being. Our souls and bodies grow into maturity. This is one of the great purposes of regeneration—to bring our body, soul, and spirit back into the original unity and harmony God designed.

It is to our free will that Paul makes his plea, *"Consider yourselves to be dead to sin. . . . Do not let sin reign in your mortal body . . . do not go on presenting the members of your body to sin as instruments of unrighteousness"* (Romans 6:11-13).

These are commands that can be ignored or followed. Our responsibility is to choose to believe and obey, and then the Spirit goes into action and pours the power into us to do what we have believed. We are never relieved of the responsibility of choosing to follow the Father's will, but the actual power to do it comes from the Holy Spirit. That is what Paul meant when he said, *"For it is God who works in you, both to will and to do"* (Philippians 2:13 NKJV).

There's a three-step progression: TRUST, OBEY, EXPECT. First, we simply trust that what God has called us to do is His best and highest plan because

He loves us. Second, in the light of that knowledge, we obey His will. Third, we expect Him to keep His end of the bargain and empower us to do His will.

The believer who consistently allows himself to be renewed in his mind and spirit by the Holy Spirit is a *"spiritual man"* (I Corinthians 3:1). This doesn't mean he is a perfect, sinless man, but he is characterized as being preoccupied with the things of God and the spirit. When he sins, he confesses it to God and quickly claims forgiveness. Then he turns again to walk by faith.

Regeneration means God has made us whole people again. He has equipped us to live victoriously in this life and gloriously with Him in eternity.

"Not by works of righteousness which we have done, but according to His mercy He saved us, through the washing of regeneration and renewing of the Holy Spirit" (Titus 3:5 NKJV).

Chapter EIGHTEEN

NEW POSITION: CREATURES OF ETERNITY LIVING IN TIME

*Y*ou don't have to be a believer long before you discover that being a Christian and living like one are often different things. As the Apostle Paul wrote of his experience in Romans chapter seven, we find that we want to do the right thing while continuing to do the very thing we hate.

The deeper, higher, victorious, abiding, exchanged, and Spirit-filled life is not an elusive, wishful aspiration. It's simply a matter of living with the moment-by-moment awareness that because of my absolute oneness with Jesus in the eyes of God, all that He is, I am. His victory over sin is my victory over sin. He's holy and blameless in the eyes of the Father and so am I. Satan no longer has any authority over Him, and he has no authority over me, either. Jesus is more than conqueror, and God's Word testifies that I am, too.

In other words, my new position in Christ gives me a total identification with Jesus in God's eyes. As He looks at the Son, He looks at me in the same way because He sees me in the Son and the Son in me.

Believers are the richest people in town! They are spiritual billionaires, if they only realize it. Paul reveals that God *"has blessed us with every spiritual blessing in the heavenly places in Christ"* (Ephesians 1:3).

Your position as a born-again Christian also means that you will never be disowned. When you are born into your earthly family, you may be a winner or loser but you're still a member of your family. There is no way to be unborn because you don't measure up to the family standards. Your earthly parents might disown you, but God never will. You will be disciplined in grace for wrong behavior, but you won't be disowned.

I read about a man who lived like a bum for many years. He had been left a huge sum of money, but the authorities couldn't locate him. They traced him from flophouse to flophouse and finally found him asleep on a fifty-cents-a-night cot in a mission. He was then informed of his inheritance. He'd been rich for years but never knew it. He had lived as a tramp needlessly.

When I heard about this I thought, "What a waste of all those years." And that's just how I feel when I think of all the wasted years that go down the drain because "believers" are "unbelievers" when it comes to taking God at His word when He tells us who we are because of whose we are.

When we fail to live in the reality of experiencing the forgiveness, freedom, acceptance, and empowering of the Spirit, we short-change ourselves and the Lord. We rob the people whose lives we touch because they need to see the reality of God in us.

Not only are my sins no longer offensive to God, but I am not, either. I am so accepted by the Father that He sees me as actually being seated in heaven with Christ. Paul emphasized this when he wrote, *"But God, being rich in mercy, because of His great love with which He loved us, even when we were dead in our transgressions, made us alive together with Christ . . . and raised us up with Him, and seated us with Him in the heavenly places in Christ Jesus"* (Ephesians 2:4-6).

If we have the notion that there is anything we can do in our own strength to improve our status with God and to resist the power of sin, then we'll miss God's solution. Many believers, including myself, have set out on rigorous programs of Bible study, prayer, scripture memorization, witnessing—and other "good religious activities"—in an effort to overcome sin and Satan's power. The results all turn out about the same. At first these activities seem to help, but gradually we end up in a cycle of failure, self-recrimination, and dedication of the flesh to try harder.

If you have come to the point where you have no more formulas left for living victoriously, then there's one thing you can do: Thank God that He's finally revealed the path to victorious Christian living to you and stand by faith on your co-crucifixion with Christ to sin's power.

When we take our stand on what God says about this, then we can expect to be delivered from sin's power. God promises, *"For sin shall not be master over you, for you are not under law, but under grace"* (Romans 6:14). Law demands and gives no help. Grace gives us the desire for God's will, then gives us the certainty of victory because our foe is defeated, and then provides the power to carry through.

If we are "sin" conscious continually, then we cannot be "Son" conscious. Sin consciousness only leads us to self-condemnation and self-effort to overcome the sin. But Son consciousness continually reminds us of God's love and acceptance of us and the forgiveness which He purchased at the cross. In short, we must focus on the problem Solver, not on the problem.

We have been anything but holy and blameless. For some, there are probably things you have not been able to forgive yourself for, let alone accept God's forgiveness for them. Paul says in Romans 12:2 that the only way to be transformed and not conform to the old way you used to behave is to have your mind renewed. Then the psalmist tells us how this is done: *"How can a young man* [and woman] *keep his way pure? By keeping it according to Thy word. . . . Thy word I have treasured in my heart, that I may not sin against Thee"* (Psalm 119:9, 11).

The world, the flesh, and the Devil don't let

up on us just because we have been born again. In fact, that's when the real conflict begins. The Devil will really work to keep you conscious of your faults and failures. He doesn't want you to see the brand new creation God has made.

When I believe and accept who God says I am in Christ, then I'll begin to behave like it. As I let the Holy Spirit renew my mind, I will begin to be transformed into His image and likeness.

I began this book with my personal story. I sought to share what a miracle it was that God pursued me and brought me into His forever family. I also wanted to show Christ as the healer of broken hearts and damaged lives. No one could have been more fouled up in his personal life than I was.

It wasn't until I learned about my new eternal position in Christ that I began to feel like a different person. No one had ever thought so highly of me. As I continued to find out more about this great God who had loved me so much that He put me into union with His Son, I had a greater appreciation of who I was because of whose I was. My Father is a King, so that makes me a member of the royal family.

As you have read this book, my sincere hope is that you have begun to see Jesus and yourself in a whole new light. If you've needed to be reconciled to God, I pray that you have been. If you've needed to be liberated from a quagmire of self-life and defeat, I trust you've seen the provision God has made for your liberation.

But most of all, I pray that you have come to see more of God's amazing grace—which was made available to you through the cross.

You were made to soar with "God's eagles." In Christ you're lifted above the damage and fetters of sin on the *"wings of eagles"* (Isaiah 40:28-31). Settle back in faith and begin to enjoy this "so great salvation" that has been all provided by God's AMAZING GRACE.

I'll see you in the heavenlies,

Hal Lindsey, saved by grace

When we've been there ten thousand years,
bright shining as the sun;
We've no less days to sing God's praise,
than when we first begun.

~CAPTAIN JOHN NEWTON

cious did tha... ...ear ☙ The hour I first be

eady come; ☙ 'Tis grace hath brought me safe thus

d to me, ☙ His Word my hope secures; ☙ He

en this flesh and heart shall fail, ☙ And mortal lif

d peace. ☙ The world shall soon dissolve like snow,

ow, ☙ Shall be forever mine. ☙ When we've been

less days to sing God's praise ☙ Than when we'd

ed a wretch like me! ☙ I once was lost, but now ar

ght my heart to fear, ☙ And grace my fears relieved

ieved. ☙ Through many dangers, toils and snares,

☙ And grace will lead me home. ☙ The Lord

l my shield and portion be, ☙ As long as life endure

shall cease, ☙ I shall possess, within the veil, ☙

The sun refuse to shine; ☙ But God, who called

re ten thousand years, ☙ Bright shining as the sun,

t begun. ☙ Amazing grace! How sweet the

eved. ❧ Through many dangers, toils and snares,
r, ❧ And grace will lead me home. ❧ The Lord
will my shield and portion be, ❧ As long as life endu
shall cease, ❧ I shall possess, within the veil, ❧
❧ The sun refuse to shine; ❧ But God, who call
here ten thousand years, ❧ Bright shining as the su
first begun . ❧ Amazing grace! How sweet the sou
found; ❧ Was blind, but now I see. ❧ Twas
❧ How precious did that grace appear ❧ The
❧ I have already come; ❧ Tis grace hath brough
as promised good to me, ❧ His Word my hope sec
❧ Yea, when this flesh and heart shall fail, ❧
A life of joy and peace. ❧ The world shall soon diss
me here below, ❧ Shall be forever mine. ❧ When
❧ We've no less days to sing God's praise ❧
That saved a wretch like me! ❧ I once was l